MOOD ENHANCING
MANDALAS
VOLUME 2

Mandala Coloring Books For
Relaxation, Meditation and Creativity

My Masterpiece
ADULT COLORING BOOKS

My Masterpiece™
Adult Coloring Books

My Masterpiece™ brings you 50 delightful illustrations to whisk you away from the world of busyness and stress and take you to that restful place where you can relax, unwind and have some fun.

We provide the creative framework and you provide the artistic imagination, using your favorite coloring implements and colors to create your own "Masterpiece".

Each illustration is on its own page so you won't experience bleed-through with colored pencils or gel pens. If you use markers, it is recommended that you place an additional piece of paper behind the illustration you are working on to help protect the next illustration.

We hope you enjoy coloring these wonderful illustrations and creating your very own "My Masterpiece".

International Standard Book Number
ISBN 13: 978-0692624852
ISBN 10: 0692624856

Share Your Masterpiece!

Post your colored pages with the hashtag: #MyMasterpieceContest on Instagram, Facebook, Twitter and Pinterest so we can show off your artistic flair.

Visit www.MyMasterpieceColoring.com to see all the ways you can enter to win great prizes in our monthly Giveaways!

Go To: www.MyMasterpieceColoring.com

Follow us on Instagram:
www.Instagram.com/MyMasterpieceColoring

Follow us on Facebook:
www.Facebook.com/MyMasterpieceColoring

Follow us on Twitter:
www.Twitter.com/MyMasterpieceCo

Follow us on Pinterest:
www.Pinterest.com/MyMasterpieces

Popular Coloring Books for Adults

My Masterpiece Adult Coloring Books - Mood Enhancing Mandalas Volume 1
Secret of the Peaceful Garden Coloring Book for Grownups (Garden Coloring Books for Adults) Volume 1
Adult Coloring Book: Stress Relieving Patterns by Blue Star Coloring
Adult Coloring Book: Stress Relieving Animal Designs by Blue Star Coloring
Creative Haven Creative Cats Coloring Book (Creative Haven Coloring Books) by Marjorie Sarnat
Creative Haven Owls Coloring Book (Creative Haven Coloring Books) by Marjorie Sarnat
Balance (Angie's Extreme Stress Menders Volume 1) by Angie Grace
Enchanted Forest: An Inky Quest & Coloring Book by Johanna Basford
Secret Garden: An Inky Treasure Hunt and Coloring Book by Johanna Basford
Color Me Calm: 100 Coloring Templates for Meditation and Relaxation (A Zen Coloring Book) by Lacy Mucklow
Lost Ocean: An Inky Adventure and Coloring Book by Johanna Basford
Tropical World: A Coloring Book Adventure by Millie Marotta
Color Me Stress-Free: Nearly 100 Coloring Templates to Unplug and Unwind (A Zen Coloring Book)
Good Vibes Coloring Book (Coloring Activity Book) by Thaneeya McArdle
Adult Coloring Books: A Coloring Book for Adults Featuring Mandalas and Henna Inspired Flowers, Animals, and Paisley Patterns
Beauty in the Bible: Adult Coloring Book by Paige Tate
Dover Creative Haven Art Nouveau Animal Designs Coloring Book (Creative Haven Coloring Books) by Marty Noble
Creative Haven Christmas Trees Coloring Book (Creative Haven Coloring Books) by Barbara Lanza
Detailed Designs and Beautiful Patterns (Sacred Mandala Designs and Patterns...) by Lilt Kids Coloring Books
Adult Coloring Book: Stress Relieving Patterns Volume 2 by Blue Star Coloring
Creative Haven Dream Doodles: A Coloring Book with a Hidden Picture Twist by Kathleen G Ahrens
Paisley Designs Coloring Book (Dover Design Coloring Books) by Marty Noble
Creative Haven Floral Frenzy (Creative Haven Coloring Books) by Miryam Adatto
Animal Kingdom: Color Me, Draw Me by Millie Marotta
The Calm Coloring Book (Chartwell Coloring Books) by Patience Coster
Adult Coloring Book: Ocean Animal Patterns by Daniela Licalzi
Creative Haven Fanciful Faces Coloring Book (Creative Haven Coloring Books) by Miryam Adatto
Dover Creative Haven Mehndi Designs Coloring Book (Creative Haven Coloring Books) by Marty Noble
Adult Coloring Book: Butterflies and Flowers : Stress Relieving Patterns (Volume 7) by Cherina Kohey
"Today Is Going To Be A Great Day" Inspirational Adult Coloring Book by Christian Art Publishers
Creative Haven Whimsical Gardens Coloring Book (Creative Haven Coloring Books) by Alexandra Cowell
Creative Haven Entangled Coloring Book (Creative Haven Coloring Books) by Dr. Angela Porter
Creative Haven Midnight Garden Coloring Book: Heart & Flower Designs on a Dramatic Black Background by Lindsey Boylan
Adult Coloring Book: Magic Christmas : for Relaxation Meditation Blessing (Volume 8) by Cherina Kohey
Color Me Happy: 100 Coloring Templates That Will Make You Smile (A Zen Coloring Book) by Lacy Mucklow and Angela Porter
Simple Blessings: Coloring Designs to Encourage Your Heart by Karla Dornacher
Fantastic Cities: A Coloring Book of Amazing Places Real and Imagined by Steve McDonald
Splendid Cities: Color Your Way to Calm by Rosie Goodwin and Alice Chadwick
Secret Paris: Color Your Way to Calm by Zoe de Las Cases
Centered (Angie's Extreme Stress Menders Volume 2) by Angie Grace
Faith in Color: An Adult Coloring Book by Pearlyn Choco and Paige Tate
The Mindfulness Coloring Book: Anti-Stress Art Therapy for Busy People by Emma Farrarons
Vive Le Color! Japan (Coloring Book): Color In: De-Stress by Abrams Noterie and Original French Edition by Marabout
Creative Haven Country Scenes Coloring Book (Creative Haven Coloring Books) by Dot Barlowe
Color Love Coloring Book: On-The-Go! by Thaneeya McArdle
Floral Bouquets Coloring Book (Dover Nature Coloring Book) by Charlene Tarbox
Color Zen Coloring Book: On-The-Go! by Valentina Harper
Creative Haven Enchanted Fairies Coloring Book (Creative Haven Coloring Books) by Barbara Lanza
The Mandala Coloring Book: Inspire Creativity, Reduce Stress, and Bring Balance with 100 Mandala Coloring Pages by Jim Gogarty
Doodle Invasion: Zifflin's Coloring Book by Zifflin and Kerby Rosanes
Tangle Wood: A Captivating Colouring Book with Hidden Jewels by Jessica Palmer
Flower Designs Coloring Book: An Adult Coloring Book for Stress-Relief, Relaxation, Meditation and Creativity by Jenean Morrison
Joyful Designs Adult Coloring Book (31 stress-relieving designs) by Joy Ting
Don't Worry, Be Happy Coloring Book Treasury: Color Your Way To A Calm, Positive Mood by Thaneeya McArdle
Creative Haven NatureScapes Coloring Book (Creative Haven Coloring Books) by Patricia J. Wynne
Goddesses Coloring Book (Dover Coloring Books) by Marty Noble
Happy Campers Coloring Book (Design Originals) (Coloring Is Fun) by Thaneeya McArdle
Really RELAXING Colouring Book 2: Colour Me Calm (Really RELAXING Colouring Books) (Volume 2) by Elizabeth James
Wonderful World of Horses Coloring Book (Dover Nature Coloring Book) by John Green
Follow Your Bliss Coloring Book (Coloring Activity Book) by Thaneeya McArdle
An Adult Coloring Book: Wild and Free: Featuring unique animal designs by Coloring Book Illustrators

More Coloring Books for Grown-Ups

Mystical Mandala Coloring Book (Dover Design Coloring Books)
Mandala Coloring Book: Stress Relieving Patterns: Coloring Books For Adults
Nature Mandalas Coloring Book (Design Originals)
The Big Book of Mandalas Coloring Book: More Than 200 Mandala Coloring Pages for Inner Peace and Inspiration
Mandala Designs Coloring Book No. 1: 35 New Mandala Designs
Creative Coloring Mandalas: Art Activity Pages to Relax and Enjoy! by Valentina Harper
Stress Less Coloring - Mandalas: 100+ Coloring Pages for Peace and Relaxation
My First Mandalas Coloring Book
The Craft of Coloring: 35 Mandala Designs: An Adult Coloring Book
The World's Best Mandala Coloring Book: A Stress Management Coloring Book For Adults
Creative Haven Nature Mandalas Coloring Book (Creative Haven Coloring Books)
Creative Haven Snowflake Mandalas Coloring Book
Coloring Mandalas 2 (Vol 2) by Susanne F. Fincher
Mandala Coloring Book Vol 3 by MJT Publishing, Penny Farthing Graphics
Coloring Beautiful Mandalas The Coloring Book For Adults by Lilt Kids Coloring Books
Mandala Design Coloring Book: Volume 1 by Jenean Morrison
Creative Haven Nature Mandalas Coloring Book by Marty Noble
Coloring Books for Grownup: Celtic Mandala Coloring Pages by Chiquita Publishing
Breathe (Angie's Extreme Stress Menders Volume 3) by Angie Grace
Coloring For Adults Beautiful Patterns & Mandalas Coloring Book
Cool (Angie's Extreme Coloring Books Volume 2) by Angie Grace
Creative Haven Paisley Mandalas Coloring Book by Shala Kerrigan
Tangle Wood: A Captivating Colouring Book with Hidden Jewels by Jessica Palmer
Colorful Cats: 30 Best Stress Relieving Cats Designs (Adult Coloring Books)
Pattern and Design Coloring Book (Volume 1) by Jenean Morrison
The Art of Zentangle: 50 inspiring drawings, designs & ideas for the meditative artist
The Affirmations Coloring Book by Louise Hay, Alberta Hutchinson
Home for the Holidays: A Hand-Crafted Adult Coloring Book by Galadrel A. L. Thompson
Color Christmas Coloring Book: Perfectly Portable Pages (On-The-Go Coloring Book)
Splendid Cities: Color Your Way to Calm by Rosie Goodwin, Alice Chadwick
Creative Haven Midnight Forest Coloring Book: Animal Designs on a Dramatic Black Background
Christmas Coloring Book (Coloring Is Fun) by Thaneeya McArdle
Christmas Designs Adult Coloring Book by Peter Pauper Press
Adult Coloring Book Designs: Stress Relief Coloring Book: Garden Designs, Mandalas, Animals, and Paisley Patterns
Mandala Magic: Amazing Mandalas Coloring Book for Adults (Color Magic)
Good Vibes Coloring Book (Coloring Is Fun) by Thaneeya McArdle
Adult Coloring Books: Mandala Coloring Book for Stress Relief by Adult Coloring Book World
Jasmine Becket-Griffith Coloring Book: A Fantasy Art Adventure by Jasmine Becket-Griffith
Adult Coloring Book: Designs by Two Hoots Coloring
Adult Coloring Book: Animal Kingdom: Animals Out The Wazoo by Two Hoots Coloring
Animorphia: An Extreme Coloring and Search Challenge by Kerby Rosanes
Adult Coloring Book: Stress Relieving Cats by Blue Star Coloring
Kaleidoscope Wonders | Color Art for Everyone - Leisure Arts by Leisure Arts
Dream Catcher: life on earth: A powerful & inspiring adult colouring book celebrating the beauty of nature by Christina Rose
Adult Coloring Book: Stress Relieving Animal Designs Volume 2 by Blue Star Coloring
Beautiful relaxation: Coloring book for everyone by Danny Dimm

Arts & Photography, Drawing, Pen & Ink, Graphic Design Techniques, Use of Color, Commercial Illustration, Pencil, Pen & Ink, Crafts, Hobbies & Home, Crafts & Hobbies, Papercrafts, Stamping & Stencil, Papercrafts, Stamping & Stenciling, Papercrafts, Techniques, Activities, Activity Books, Activities, Crafts & Games, Arts & Photography, Coloring Books for Grown-Ups, Children's Books, Crafts & Games, Decorative Arts & Design, Plants & Animals, Alternative Medicine, Meditation, Book Design, Humor & Entertainment, Pop Culture, Art, Puzzles & Games, Religion & Spirituality, New Age & Spirituality

Need more mandala coloring books? Try looking up these other categories:

adult mandala coloring book
color books for girls
mandala color book
mandala color books
mandala coloring book adults
color book for girls
color book for teens
color books for teens
mandala coloring books for teens
mandala coloring book for teens
mandala coloring book for grownups
mandala coloring books for grownups
mandala coloring book for everyone
mandala coloring books for everyone
mandala coloring book for men
mandala coloring books for men
mandala coloring book for boys
mandala coloring books for boys
mandala coloring book for teenagers
mandala coloring books for teenagers
mandala coloring books for meditation
mandala coloring books adults
mandala coloring book advanced
mandala coloring books advanced
mandala coloring book cheap
mandala coloring book difficult
mandala coloring book design originals
mandala coloring book everyone
mandala coloring book girl
mandala coloring book large
mandala coloring book men
mandala coloring book prime
mandala coloring books prime
mandala coloring book teens
mandala coloring books teens
mandala coloring book zen
mandala coloring books zen
mandala coloring books to relax
mandala coloring books best sellers
mandala color book for adults
mandala color books for adults
mandala color book for grownups
mandala color books for grownups
color books for teen girls
color book for teen girls
color book for grownups
color books for grownups
adult coloring books amazon prime
adult coloring books
coloring books for adults

mandala coloring pages
adult coloring
coloring book for adults
coloring for adults
mandala designs
hard coloring pages
mandalas to color
abstract coloring pages
mandala coloring
adult coloring book pages
amazon adult coloring books
adult coloring sheets
adult coloring page
free mandala coloring pages
intricate coloring pages
coloring mandalas
coloring sheets for adults
best mandala coloring book
adult color books
color pages for adults
mandala design
adult color pages
pattern coloring pages
complex coloring pages
mandalas coloring
difficult coloring books for adults
advanced coloring books
complex coloring books for adults
best coloring books for adults
mandalas coloring book
mandala images
complicated coloring pages
mandalas for kids
coloring pages adults
mandalas coloring pages
adult coloring pages mandala
printable mandala coloring pages
adults coloring books
easy mandala
adult colouring books
mandala pictures
mystical mandala coloring book
coloring pages mandala
coloring pages adult
mandalas to color
mandala book
adult colouring book
coloring mandala
therapeutic coloring pages
coloring book adults

coloring books adults
top coloring books for adults
simple mandalas
simple mandala designs
mandala to color
mandala books
colouring books for adults
best adult coloring books
cool mandalas
advanced mandala coloring pages
intricate coloring books
cool coloring books for adults
challenging coloring pages for adults
easy mandalas
cool design coloring pages
the mandala coloring book
adult coloring images
simple mandala coloring pages
mandela coloring pages
awesome coloring books for adults
intricate coloring books
colouring book for adults
mandala color pages
adults coloring pages
easy mandala coloring pages
colouring pages for adults
mandala sheets
mandala templates
mandalas for adults
mandalas to color for adults
adult color page
mandala simple
complicated coloring pages for adults
mandalas for coloring
extreme coloring pages
coloring books for seniors
coloring adult
mandala coloring pages for kids
amazon prime coloring books
mandala designs to color
difficult coloring pages
abstract coloring page
adult coloring designs
mandela coloring
therapy coloring pages
coloring pages for adults
coloring pages for kids
adult coloring pages
adult coloring book
best selling coloring books for adults

www.ingramcontent.com/pod-product-compliance
Lightning Source LLC
Chambersburg PA
CBHW081216020426
42331CB00012B/3038